# Aimee and the Table

Written by Tom Pinfield

Illustrated by Elisa Rocchi

Collins

Mum looks on the tablet.

Aimee sits with her.

Aimee has a turn.

A box appears.

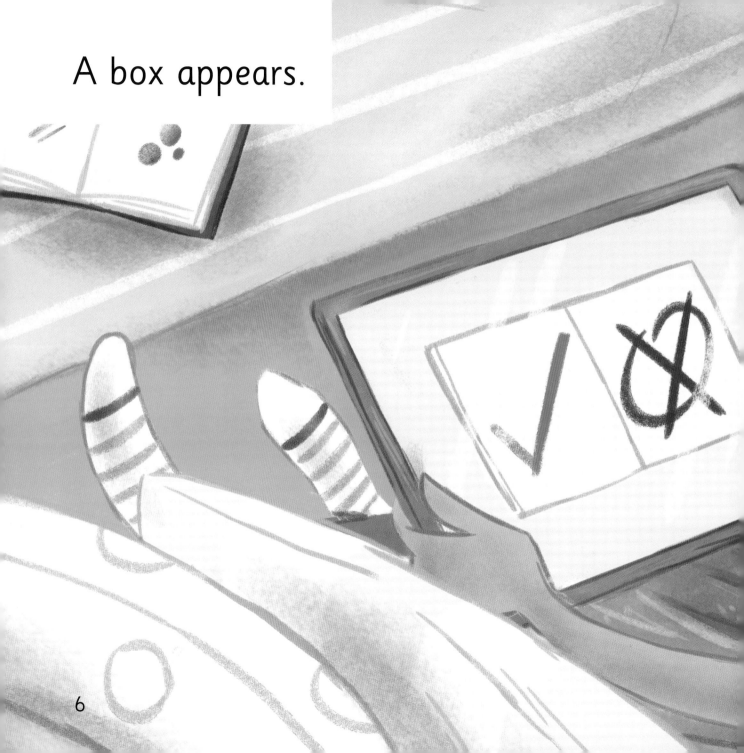

Aimee has a think.

Aimee needs to check with Mum.

It is all better now.

13

# Aimee and the tablet

#  After reading

**Letters and Sounds:** Phase 3

**Word count:** 59

**Focus phonemes:** /ai/ /ee/ /igh/ /oa/ /oo/ /oo/ /ur/ /ow/ /ear/ /er/

**Common exception words:** to, the, all

**Curriculum links:** Understanding the World

**Early learning goals:** Reading: read and understand simple sentences; use phonic knowledge to decode regular words and read them aloud accurately

## Developing fluency

- Challenge your child to read the sentence on each left-hand page, while you read the right-hand pages. Demonstrate reading the speech bubbles in a voice for Aimee.
- Swap roles, encouraging your child to read the right-hand pages, and the speech bubbles in a voice for Aimee.

## Phonic practice

- Remind your child that two letters together can make just one sound. Ask your child to sound out, then blend these words:

  n/ow      l/oo/k/s      t/ur/n/      g/oa/t      Ai/m/ee

- Remind your child that sometimes three letters can together make just one sound. Ask them to sound out, then blend these words:

  r/igh/t      a/pp/ear/s

## Extending vocabulary

- Ask your child to think of two meanings for each of these words:
  - **turn** (e.g. go, *move round*)
  - **tablet** (e.g. *computer, pill*)
  - **cool** (e.g. *really good, a bit cold*)